D0614941

DEEPENING
LIFE
TOGETHER

PRAYING GOD'S WAY

LIFE TOGETHER

BakerBooks
a division of Baker Publishing Group
Grand Rapids, Michigan

© 2009 by Lifetogether Publishing

Published by Baker Books
a division of Baker Publishing Group
P.O. Box 6287, Grand Rapids, MI 49516-6287
www.bakerbooks.com

Printed in the United States of America

Library of Congress Cataloging-in-Publication Data
Praying God's way / [editors, Mark L. Strauss, Teresa Haymaker].
    p.   cm. — (Deepening life together)
    Includes bibliographical references.
    ISBN 978-0-8010-6847-8 (pbk.)
    1. Prayer—Christianity—Textbooks. 2. Prayer—Christianity—Study and teaching.
I. Strauss, Mark L. II. Haymaker, Teresa.
    BV215.P765 2009
    248.3'2—dc22   2009014725

CONTENTS

Contents

ACKNOWLEDGMENTS

The *Deepening Life Together: Praying God's Way* Small Group Video Bible Study has come together through the efforts of many at Baker Publishing Group, Lifetogether Publishing, and Lamplighter Media, for which we express our heartfelt thanks.

Executive Producer	John Nill
Producer and Director	Sue Doc Ross
Editors	Mark L. Strauss (Scholar), Teresa Haymaker
Curriculum Development	Brett Eastman, Caroline Erickson, Sue Doc Ross, Stephanie French, Teresa Haymaker, Mark L. Strauss, Karen Lee-Thorp
Video Production	Chris Balish, Rodney Bissell, Nick Calabrese, Sebastian Hoppe Fuentes, Josh Greene, Patrick Griffin, Teresa Haymaker, Oziel Jabin Ibarra, Natali Ibarra, Janae Janik, Keith Sorrell, Lance Tracy
Teachers and Scholars	Andrew Hill, John Hutchinson, Jon Laansma, George McKinney, Nick Perrin, Mark Strauss, Daniel Watson
Baker Publishing	Jack Kuhatschek

Special thanks to DeLisa Ivy, Bethel Seminary, Talbot School of Theology, Wheaton College

Clips from The JESUS Film are copyright © 1995–2009 The JESUS Film Project®. A ministry of Campus Crusade for Christ International®.

Interior icons by Tom Clark

READ ME FIRST

Most people want to live a healthy, balanced spiritual life, but few achieve this by themselves. And most small groups struggle to balance all of God's purposes in their meetings. Groups tend to overemphasize one of the five purposes, perhaps fellowship or discipleship. Rarely is there a healthy balance that includes evangelism, ministry, and worship. That's why we've included all of these elements in this study so you can live a healthy, balanced spiritual life over time.

A typical group session will include the following:

Memory Verses

For each session we have provided a memory verse that emphasizes an important truth from the session. This is an optional exercise, but we believe that memorizing Scripture can be a vital part of filling our minds with God's Word. We encourage you to give this important habit a try.

CONNECTING *with God's Family (Fellowship)*

The foundation for spiritual growth is an intimate connection with God and his family. A few people who really know you and who earn your trust provide a place to experience the life Jesus invites you to live. This section of each session typically offers you two activities. You can get to know your whole group by using the icebreaker question, and/or you can check in with one or two group members—your spiritual partner(s)—for a deeper connection and encouragement in your spiritual journey.

DVD TEACHING SEGMENT. A *Deepening Life Together: Praying God's Way* Video Teaching DVD companion to this study guide is available. For each study session, the DVD contains a lesson taught by George McKinney. If you are using the DVD, you will view the teaching segment after your *Connecting* discussion and before your group discussion time (the *Growing* section). At the end of each session in this study guide you will find space for your notes on the teaching segment.

GROWING *to Be Like Christ (Discipleship)*

Here is where you come face-to-face with Scripture. In core passages you'll explore what the Bible teaches about the topic of the study. The focus won't be on accumulating information but on how we should live in light of the Word of God. We want to help you apply the Scriptures practically, creatively, and from your heart as well as your head. At the end of the day, allowing the timeless truths from God's Word to transform our lives in Christ is our greatest aim.

DEVELOPING *Your Gifts to Serve Others (Ministry)*

Jesus trained his disciples to discover and develop their gifts to serve others. And God has designed each of us uniquely to serve him in a way no other person can. This section will help you discover and use your God-given design. It will also encourage your group to discover your unique design as a community. In this study, you'll put into practice what you've learned in the Bible study by taking a step to serve others. These simple steps will take your group on a faith journey that could change your lives forever.

SHARING *Your Life Mission Every Day (Evangelism)*

Many people skip over this aspect of the Christian life because it's scary, relationally awkward, or simply too much work for their busy schedules. But Jesus wanted all of his disciples to help outsiders connect with him, to know him personally. This doesn't mean preaching on street corners. It could mean welcoming a few newcomers into your group, hosting a short-term group in your home, or walking through this study with a friend. In this study, you'll have an opportunity to go beyond Bible study to biblical living.

SURRENDERING *Your Life for God's Pleasure (Worship)*

God is most pleased by a heart that is fully his. Each group session will give you a chance to surrender your heart to God in prayer and worship. You may read a psalm together, share a page in your journal, or sing a song to close your meeting. If you have never prayed aloud in a group before, no one will pressure you. Instead, you'll experience the support of others who are praying for you.

Study Notes

This section provides background notes on the Bible passage(s) you examine in the *Growing* section. You may want to refer to these notes during your group meeting or as a reference for those doing additional study.

For Deeper Study (Optional)

If you want to dig deeper into more Bible passages about the topic at hand, we've provided additional passages and questions. Your group may choose to do study homework ahead of each meeting in order to cover more biblical material. Or you as an individual may choose to study the *For Deeper Study* on your own. If you prefer not to do study homework, the *Growing* section will provide you with plenty to discuss within the group. These options allow individuals or the whole group to go deeper in their study, while still accommodating those who can't do homework or are new to your group.

You can record your discoveries in your journal. We encourage you to read some of your insights to a friend (spiritual partner) for accountability and support. Spiritual partners may check in each week over the phone, through e-mail, or at the beginning of the group meeting.

Reflections

On the *Reflections* pages we provide Scriptures to read and reflect on between group meetings. We suggest you use this section to seek God at home throughout the week. This time at home should begin and end with prayer. Don't get in a hurry; take enough time to hear God's direction.

Subgroup for Discussion and Prayer

If your group is large (more than seven people), we encourage you to separate into groups of two to four for discussion and prayer. This is to encourage greater participation and deeper discussion.

INTRODUCTION

Welcome to the *Deepening Life Together* Bible study on *Praying God's Way*. Our relationship with God is strengthened and our knowledge of him grows as we share our lives with him in prayer. Jesus made prayer the highest priority in his life, turning to God not only in times of crisis, but in times of decision, need, and joy and happiness as well. Jesus shared his whole life with God, not just the difficult or challenging parts.

In this study we will learn to pray as Jesus prayed as we experience Scripture together. This journey will make known God's purposes for our prayer lives. We will connect with our loving and faithful Father and with other believers in small group community. We will become his hands and feet here on earth as he reveals our uniqueness and his willingness to use us. And we will experience the closeness that he desires with us as we prayerfully respond to him and learn to place him first in our lives.

We at Baker Books and Lifetogether Publishing look forward to hearing the stories of how God changes you from the inside out during this small group experience. We pray God blesses you with all he has planned for you through this journey together.

> For the LORD is good and his love endures forever;
> his faithfulness continues through all generations.
>
> Psalm 100:5 (NIV)

THE PRIORITY OF PRAYER
STAYING CONNECTED 24/7

Memory Verse: Before daybreak the next morning, Jesus got up and went out to an isolated place to pray (Mark 1:35 NLT).

In this digital age, the term "staying connected" conjures up images of cell phones, text messaging, e-mail, e-greetings, blogs, and Facebook—to name a few. We communicate with our families, coworkers, classmates, and loved ones, both near and far away, with handheld devices or computers, without even the need to pick up a telephone.

One would think with all the technology, we would have more free time; but realistically, we have less. Our days are so full that we still fail to keep in touch with people we care about, much less the One who deserves our attention the most—our heavenly Father.

We can learn much from the fact that, despite an impossibly busy schedule, Jesus made time to be quiet and alone with God, his Father. He knew that above all else, he needed to keep connected to his source of strength and guidance. We all need this connection as well. Thankfully, Jesus invites us to partner with him and discover the joy of staying connected to him 24 hours a day, seven days a week.

Connecting

Open your group with prayer. Ask the Lord to unify your group and challenge you as you study about prayer through this study.

Take time to pass around a copy of the *Small Group Roster*, a sheet of paper, or one of you pass your study guide, opened to the *Small Group Roster*. Each of you write down your contact information including the best time and method for contacting you. Then, someone volunteer to make copies or type up a list with everyone's information and e-mail it to the group this week.

1. Begin this first session of *Praying God's Way* by introducing yourselves. Include your name, what you do for a living, and what you do for fun. You may also include whether or not you are married, how long you have been married, how many children you have, and their ages.

2. Whether your group is new or ongoing, it's always important to reflect on and review your group values together. In the *Appendix* is a *Small Group Agreement* with the values we've found most useful in sustaining healthy, balanced groups. Choose two or three values that you have room to grow in, or haven't previously focused on, to emphasize during this study. Doing this will take your group to the next stage of intimacy and spiritual health.

3. Share your expectations for this study on prayer. How do you hope God will challenge you?

Growing

Jesus made prayer the highest priority in his life. Many times in the Bible we see Jesus setting aside time to be alone with God despite a hectic schedule. We will discuss how Jesus handled his busyness, what kinds of things he prayed about, and why.

14

4. Read Mark 1:14–34. Jesus had a very busy ministry. What kinds of things occupied his time?

   How are these things like or unlike the things that occupy your daily life?

5. Mark 1:35 shows us that, as busy as he was, Jesus took time to pray to his heavenly Father. Read Mark 1:35 aloud. Where did Jesus go to pray?

   What do you think is the significance of where Jesus prayed?

6. Read Mark 1:36–39. What do you think was the connection between Jesus's decision to make time for prayer and the way he dealt with people's expectations?

7. Jesus's busy schedule wasn't about to change anytime soon. How do you respond to this statement: "If we are too busy to pray, we are too busy"?

8. What are some of the things that sometimes hinder you from prayer?

9. Look up the following passages and note how prayer fit into Jesus's life and ministry at various points. For instance, what did he pray about? What happened when he prayed?
   ☐ Luke 3:21–22
   ☐ Luke 9:28–31
   ☐ Luke 6:12–13
   ☐ Luke 22:41–44; 23:46

10. How would you summarize the role prayer played in Jesus's life?

11. Do you think Jesus was unique in his need for consistent times of prayer? Explain.

12. What will it take for you to build consistent times of prayer into your life?

How motivated are you to do this? Why is that?

Jesus made prayer the highest priority in his life, knowing that he could only accomplish his mission through complete dependence on the Father. It is so with us as well. Prayer is the primary means by which we stay connected to the Father, Jesus, and the Holy Spirit. And apart from that connection, we can do nothing (John 15:5).

 Developing

God has designed each of us uniquely with individual talents, abilities, passions, and experiences that determine where we serve within the body of Christ. Before we begin this journey of discovering how God made us, it's important to be sure that we live consistently and honestly. One way we can do this is through spiritual accountability.

13. We strongly recommend each of you partner with someone in the group to help you in your spiritual journey during this study. This person will be your "spiritual partner" for the next several weeks. Pair up with someone in your group now (men partner with men and women with women) and turn to the *Personal Health Plan.*

    In the box that says, "WHO are you connecting with spiritually?" write your partner's name. In the box that says, "WHAT is your next step for growth?" write one step you would like to take for growth during this study. Tell your partner what step you chose. When you check in with your partner each meeting, the "Partner's Progress" column on this chart will provide a place to record your partner's progress in the goal he or she chose.

Sharing

Believers are called to strengthen and encourage one another as we live out our faith each day: "And let us consider how we may spur one another on toward love and good deeds. Let us not give up meeting together, as some are in the habit of doing, but let us encourage one another—and all the more as you see the Day approaching (Heb. 10:24–25 NIV). This should include reaching out to believers around us who are not connected in a Christian community.

14. Use the *Circles of Life* diagram below to help you think of people you come in contact with on a regular basis who need to be connected in Christian community. Try to write two names in each circle. Consider the following ideas for reaching out to one or two of the people you list and make a plan to follow through with them this week.

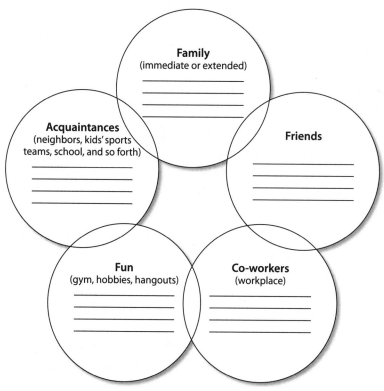

☐ This is a wonderful time to welcome a few friends into your group. Which of the people on your list could you invite? It's possible that you may need to help your friend overcome obstacles to coming to a place where he or she can encounter Jesus. Does your friend need a ride to the group or help with child care? How can you help?

☐ Consider inviting a friend to attend a weekend church service with you and possibly plan to enjoy a meal together afterward. This can be a great opportunity to talk with someone about your faith in Jesus.

☐ Is there someone who is unable to attend your group but who still needs a connection? Would you be willing to have lunch or coffee with that person, catch up on life, and share something you've learned from this study? Jesus doesn't call all of us to lead small groups, but he does call every disciple to spiritually multiply his or her life over time.

 Surrendering

Every session we will make it our priority to surrender our hearts in worship to God and to pray for one another.

15. Allow everyone to answer this question: "How can we pray for you this week?" Share your prayer requests in your group and ask everyone to write down the personal requests of each member on the *Prayer and Praise Report*. Commit to praying for your group throughout the week.

16. Take a few minutes to talk about what it would take to make time with God a priority every day or even five or six days a week. Don't demand an hour or even a half-hour of time at first; consider drawing near to God for a few minutes each day and gradually you will desire more. At the end of each session, you'll find *Reflections* pages. These include five daily Scripture readings with room to record your thoughts and space to summarize what God has taught you through the session

on day six. These will offer reinforcement of the principles we are learning and help to develop the habit of time alone with God.

Study Notes

Holy Spirit: The third Person in the Trinity. The Holy Spirit is a person distinct from the Father and the Son, though united to both in the oneness of the Godhead. In Scripture, the Holy Spirit is distinctly called God, and names are given to him that belong only to God (see Acts 5:3–4 and 28:25–27, Heb. 10:15–17, and 2 Cor. 3:17–18). Scripture also assigns divine attributes, such as knowledge, sovereignty, and eternity to the Holy Spirit (see 1 Cor. 2:11; 12:11 and Heb. 9:14). Additionally, divine works, such as creation and the new birth, are attributed to the Holy Spirit in Genesis 1:2; Job 26:13, and John 3:3–8, and homage appropriate only to God is given to the Holy Spirit in Acts 28:25–27 and 2 Corinthians 13:14.

Transfiguration: Means to "change into another form." The transfiguration of Jesus is recorded in Matthew 17:2 and Mark 9:2. In these accounts, Jesus "was transfigured" before his disciples Peter, James, and John. Jesus's external appearance was changed, his face gleaming like the sun, and his clothing being so white that it shone like light. The Transfiguration represents Jesus's glory at the right hand of God (Acts 2:33) and the glory he will have at his second coming to establish his Kingdom: *the Son of Man coming in his kingdom* (see Matt. 16:28 and 2 Peter 1:16–18). The transfiguration encouraged the disciples in the expectation of the messianic kingdom promised to Israel as the preaching of the kingdom was fast approaching its end and culmination in the rejection and imminent death of the King.

For Deeper Study (Optional)

Realizing that his time on earth was short, Jesus took the time to offer a powerful intercessory prayer to his Father in John 17:1–26. Read this prayer. What specific things did Jesus pray for:

- himself (vv. 1–5)
- his disciples (vv. 6–19)
- future believers (we are included in this) (vv. 20–26)

1. What does this prayer teach us about what a believer's prayer life should look like?

2. Read Hebrews 7:25. What does Jesus live to do for us?

3. What does that say about the value of prayer?

Reflections

Each day, read the daily verses and give prayerful consideration to what you learn about God, his Spirit, and his place in your life. Then record your thoughts, insights, or prayer in the *Reflect* section below the verses you read. On the sixth day record a summary of what you have learned through the session.

Day 1. But Jesus often withdrew to lonely places and prayed (Luke 5:16 NIV).

REFLECT

_____

_____

_____

_____

Day 2. Listen to my voice in the morning, LORD. Each morning I bring my requests to you and wait expectantly (Ps. 5:3 NLT).

REFLECT

_____

_____

_____

_____

Day 3. O LORD, I cry out to you. I will keep on pleading day by day (Ps. 88:13 NLT).

REFLECT

_____

_____

_____

_____

Day 4. Remain in me, and I will remain in you. No branch can bear fruit by itself; it must remain in the vine. Neither can you bear fruit unless you remain in me (John 15:4 NIV).

REFLECT

_____

_____

_____

_____

Day 5. Always be joyful. Never stop praying. Be thankful in all circumstances, for this is God's will for you who belong to Christ Jesus (1 Thess. 5:16–18 NLT).

REFLECT

_____

_____

_____

_____

Day 6. Use the following space to write any thoughts God has put in your heart and mind about the things we have looked at in this session and during your *Reflections* time this week.

SUMMARY

_____

_____

_____

_____

THE PATTERN OF PRAYER

Memory Verse: Your kingdom come. Your will be done on earth as it is in heaven (Matt. 6:10 NKJV).

George Mueller was a praying man. Having empty pockets, but being rich in prayer, and through God's provision, he founded five large orphan homes that cared for thousands of children in the 1800s.

"One morning the plates and cups and bowls on the table were empty. There was no food in the [pantry], and no money to buy food. The children were standing waiting for their morning meal, when Mueller said, 'Children, you know we must be in time for school.' Lifting his hand he said, 'Dear Father, we thank Thee for what Thou art going to give us to eat.' There was a knock on the door. The baker stood there, and said, 'Mr. Mueller, I couldn't sleep last night. Somehow I felt you didn't have bread for breakfast and the Lord wanted me to send you some. So I got up at 2:00 a.m. and baked some fresh bread, and have brought it.' Mueller thanked the man. No sooner had this transpired when there was a second knock at the door. It was the milkman. He announced that his milk cart had broken down right in front of the orphanage, and he would like to give the children his cans of fresh milk so he could empty his wagon and repair it. No wonder, years later, when Mueller was to travel the world as an evangelist, he would be heralded as "the man who gets things from God!"*

Mr. Mueller's simple prayer exhibits the healthy and effective pattern of prayer that Jesus taught his disciples in the "Lord's Prayer."

Connecting

Open your group with prayer. Ask for the Lord's direction and provision as you study his Word today.

1. Share briefly one situation for which you prayed and how you saw God answer.

2. Sit with your spiritual partner. If your partner is absent or if you are new to the group, join with another pair or someone who doesn't yet have a partner. (If you haven't established your spiritual partnerships yet, turn to the *Leader's Notes, Developing* section for *Session One* in the *Appendix* for information on how to begin your partnerships.)

Growing

In the Lord's Prayer in Matthew 6:9–13, we find the purpose and pattern for the kind of prayer that connects us with God. Read the full passage below and then discuss the questions that follow.

> Pray, then, in this way:
> "Our Father who is in heaven,
> Hallowed be Your name.
> Your kingdom come.
> Your will be done,
> On earth as it is in heaven.
> Give us this day our daily bread.
> And forgive us our debts, as we also have forgiven our debtors.
> And do not lead us into temptation, but deliver us from evil."
>
> Matthew 6:9–13 (NASB)

* 1. Ed Reese, *The Life and Ministry of George Mueller* (Lansing, IL: Reese Publications, n.d.).

3. Verse 9 begins by telling us that "in this way" we should pray. This indicates that this is a model for prayer rather than a prayer to be recited. What might it mean to treat these words as a model for prayer?

4. What do you think is the point of starting the way the first sentence of this prayer (v. 9) starts?

   How does this sentence acknowledge God's greatness?

   How would a habit of acknowledging God's greatness affect you?

5. Read verse 10 aloud. What is God's kingdom? See the *Study Notes* for additional insight.

   When we pray your kingdom come, what are we asking for?

   What do you think is God's plan and purpose for his kingdom?

6. Focus on the word "daily" in verse 11. Why does the Father want us to bring our needs to him daily? (See Matt. 6:25, 32–33 for help.)

7. What are the debts referred to in verse 12?

   How does asking God for forgiveness keep us connected to him spiritually?

8. How does our way of dealing with others (v. 12b) affect how God deals with us? See Matthew 6:14–15 for insight.

   Why do you think Jesus so strongly emphasizes the connection between forgiving and being forgiven?

9. Temptation in verse 13 does not mean "enticement." It means "testing." With this in mind, what is this part of the prayer about?

10. How would you use this prayer as a model if you were in the midst of suffering?

11. What are the key things you learn from this model for prayer?

Jesus's model for prayer, the Lord's Prayer, teaches us that prayer glorifies God and provides a way for believers to ask for God's provision and protection. Praying daily using this model will teach us to depend fully on God.

Developing

As our relationships with God deepen, we will discover that he empowers us to serve others with greater depth and purpose.

12. In your *Personal Health Plan*, in the "Develop" section, answer the WHERE question: "WHERE are you serving?" If you are not currently serving, note one area where you will consider serving within the small group or in the church.

13. First Peter 4:10 says: "As each one has received a gift, minister it to one another, as good stewards of the manifold grace of God" (NKJV). Every believer has been given at least one spiritual gift to use in ministry to one another. Have you discovered what your spiritual gifts are? Read through the *Spiritual Gifts Inventory* in the *Appendix* at home before the next meeting and prayerfully consider which gifts you believe God has given you. Ask a significant person in your life what they see in you as well. Understanding these gifts will help you to plug into the ministry that God has for you. This is an important step in developing your gifts to serve others. We will refer to this home exercise again in *Session Three*.

Sharing

Jesus wants all of his disciples to help nonbelievers connect with him, to know him personally. This section will provide you an opportunity to go beyond Bible study to biblical living.

14. Return to the *Circles of Life* and review the names of those you chose to invite to this group, to church, or for one-on-one discipleship. Share how your invitations went. If you are attending this group for the first time because someone invited you, feel free to share your perspective on this question.

    If you haven't followed through, think about what is preventing you from doing so. As a group, consider some ways to overcome obstacles or excuses that keep us from reaching out and inviting people into our Christian community.

Surrendering

God is most pleased by a heart that is fully his. Now, and at the end of every session, we will provide you an opportunity to surrender your hearts to God in prayer and worship.

15. Share your prayer requests in your group. Be sure to write down the personal requests of the members to use as a reminder to pray for your group at home between group meetings.

Study Notes

The Kingdom of God: The Kingdom of God embraces all of creation, both in heaven and on earth. Those who respond to God in faith and obedience enter the Kingdom and come into fellowship with him. While the Kingdom of God is present in that God is eternally the sovereign Lord of the universe, the Kingdom will come in fullness in the future, when God restores creation to it original perfection and brings everything into submission to his will.

For Deeper Study (Optional)

By examining the recorded prayers of the apostles and believers in the early Church, our own prayers will be enriched.

1. How did Paul pray for the believers in Philippians 1:9–11?

2. In Philippians 4:6, what things did Paul encourage us to pray about?

   ☐ What results when we do this?

3. Paul prayed for the Colossians in 1:9–12.

   ☐ What specifically did he ask for them (v. 9)? Why might this be important to the believer?

   ☐ What does Paul say a believer gains by being filled with the knowledge of God's will through spiritual wisdom and understanding?

   ☐ What does it mean to "live a life worthy of the Lord?"

4. What did the early church pray about in:

   ☐ Acts 1:24–25

   ☐ Acts 4:29–30

   ☐ Acts 12:5

5. What do these prayers teach us about the prayer life of a believer today?

Reflections

Each day, read the daily verses and give prayerful consideration to what you learn about God, his Spirit, and his place in your life. Then record your thoughts, insights, or prayer in the *Reflect* section below the verses you read. On the sixth day record a summary of what you have learned through this session.

Day 1. Seek the Kingdom of God above all else, and live righteously, and he will give you everything you need (Matt. 6:33 NLT).

REFLECT

_____

_____

_____

_____

Day 2. Father, if you are willing, take this cup from me; yet not my will, but yours be done (Luke 22:42 NIV).

REFLECT

_____

_____

_____

_____

Day 3. Keep falsehood and lies far from me; give me neither poverty nor riches, but give me only my daily bread (Prov. 30:8 NIV).

REFLECT

_____

_____

_____

_____

Day 4. For if you forgive men when they sin against you, your heavenly Father will also forgive you (Matt. 6:14 NIV).

REFLECT

_____

_____

_____

_____

Day 5. We know that no one who is born of God sins; but He who was born of God keeps him, and the evil one does not touch him (1 John 5:18 NASB).

REFLECT

_____

_____

_____

_____

Day 6. Use the following space to write any thoughts God has put in your heart and mind about the things we have looked at in this session and during your *Reflections* time this week.

SUMMARY

_____

_____

_____

_____

THE POWER OF PRAYER
WHATEVER YOU ASK IN MY NAME

Memory Verse: Yes, ask me for anything in my name, and I will do it! (John 14:14 NLT).

Things looked grim for the sailing ship drifting into sunken reefs off the coast of a small island in the Pacific. There was no wind and native cannibals waited on the shore. The captain and crew had given up. There was nothing left to do.

A young man on board, J. Hudson Taylor, cried to the captain, "No, there is one thing we haven't done. Four of us are Christians. Let us go to our cabins to agree in prayer and ask the Lord to give us a breeze immediately."

Minutes later, Mr. Hudson returned on deck, assured that God had answered his prayer. Finding the first officer, he implored him to let down the corners of the main sail. With contempt the officer cursed, "Nonsense! You can't pray up a wind!" But soon the topmost sail began to tremble. A good breeze! The astonished crew let down the mainsail and off they sailed.

J. Hudson Taylor went on to found the China Inland Mission that included 205 mission stations and 125,000 Chinese Christians. Of this and other similar experiences, Mr. Taylor wrote, "Thus

God encouraged me, ere landing on China's shores, to bring every variety of need to him in prayer, and to expect that he would honor the name of the Lord Jesus." Hudson had discovered the power of praying in Jesus's name.

Connecting

Prayer is powerful! It is not, however, because of the greatness of our prayers. Rather, it is because of the greatness of our God. Open your group with prayer, thanking him for the power of his name.

1. Check in with your spiritual partner, or with another partner if yours is absent. Talk about any challenges you are currently facing in reaching the goals you set during this study. Tell your spiritual partner how he or she has helped you follow through with each step. Be sure to record your progress.

2. Also begin to talk about what's next for your group. Do you want to continue meeting together? If so, the *Small Group Agreement* can help you talk through any changes you might want to make as you move forward. Consider what you will study, who will lead, and where and when you will meet.

Growing

Prayer aligns us with the will of God, and in so doing it allows us to tap into the power of the sovereign Creator of the universe. God gives us this wonderful promise: *He will answer our prayers!*

3. What three things does God encourage us to do in Matthew 7:7–8?

   How will God respond?

4. In Matthew 7:9–11, how does Jesus underscore the point he has just made in the previous verses?

How easy is if for you to see the Father as a good parent who longs to give you good gifts and is eager for you to ask, seek, and knock? Why is that?

5. What promise does Jesus make in John 14:12–14?

What reason does he give for keeping that promise?

6. What does it mean to pray in Jesus's name? See John 15:7–8, 1 John 5:14, and the *Study Notes* for insight.

7. What, then, are we to make of the fact that we often ask for very good things and don't get them?

8. Read Matthew 26:36–46. This scene takes place right before Jesus is arrested, tortured, and killed. What does Jesus ask for?

Does the Father say yes to his request? What happens?

What can we learn from this scene about praying in Jesus's name and according to the Father's will?

What can we learn from this scene about boldly asking, seeking, and knocking, knowing that the Father longs to give good gifts to his children?

9. What will you take away from this discussion?

Jesus teaches that prayer is the most potent tool in the Christian's toolbox, because it taps into the power of the sovereign Creator of the universe. God's power is within reach of every believer. To see God's power released through our prayers requires that we ask in faith, ask in Jesus's name, and ask according to his will. It is only when we are aligned with God's will that we have access to God's infinite power through prayer. Often, aligning with God's will requires deep trust in the Father's goodness.

Developing

10. Developing our ability to serve God and others according to the leading of the Holy Spirit takes time and persistence in getting to know our Lord. We must take time in prayer, in God's Word, and in meditation, to let God speak to us daily. Which steps have you taken and what kind of progress do you feel you have made? Are there any steps you would like to add?

11. During the last session, you were asked to review the *Spiritual Gifts Inventory*. Which of the spiritual gifts do you feel God has given you? What type of service to your small group or church body would allow you to best use your spiritual gifts? Commit to taking a small first step and be willing to let God lead you to the ministry that expresses your passion.

Sharing

John 17:20 says: "My prayer is not for them alone. I pray also for those who will believe in me through their message" (NIV). Jesus not only prayed for his disciples, but he prayed for the nonbelievers who would hear and accept the message. We too should make it a priority to pray for nonbelievers.

12. Return to the *Circles of Life* diagram and identify one or two people in each area of your life who need to know Christ. Write their names outside the circles for this exercise. Commit to praying for God's guidance and an opportunity to share with each of them.

13. Inviting people to church or Bible study is one way that we shepherd others toward faith in Christ. On your *Personal Health Plan*, in the "Sharing" section, answer the "WHEN are you shepherding another person in Christ?" question.

14. If you have never invited Jesus to take control of your life, why not ask him in now? If you are not clear about God's gift of eternal life for everyone who believes in Jesus and how to receive this gift, take a minute to pray and ask God to help you understand what he wants you to do about trusting in Jesus.

Surrendering

Prayer has no power without connection to the God of the universe. An important way to connect with God is through worshiping with other believers.

15. Share your praises and prayer requests with one another. Record these on the *Prayer and Praise Report*.

Study Notes

Praying in Jesus's Name: To pray in Jesus's name is to pray consistent with who he is, with the goal of bringing God glory. Praying according to God's will not only brings glory to God, but also joy to believers (John 16:23–24). When obedient believers delight themselves in the Lord, he will plant the desires in their hearts for what glorifies him (Ps. 37:4), and those desires will control their prayers. God's answers to those prayers will glorify him, bring believers' wills into line with his purposes, and fill them with joy.

For Deeper Study (Optional)

It is not only important to pray individually; it is also important to participate in corporate prayer with other believers. Study the following passages to gain a greater understanding of the importance of praying in Jesus's name.

1. What does Jesus teach us about the effectiveness of corporate prayer in Matthew 18:19–20?

2. Read John 15:7. What does Jesus say is required to receive whatever we wish? What does it mean to remain (or abide) in Jesus?

3. What example does Elijah's prayer set for us in James 5:17–18?

Reflections

Each day, read the daily verses and give prayerful consideration to what you learn about God, his Spirit, and his place in your life. Then record your thoughts, insights, or prayer in the *Reflect* section below the verses you read. On the sixth day record a summary of what you have learned through this session.

Day 1. Truly, truly, I say to you, if you ask the Father for anything in My name, He will give it to you. Until now you have asked for nothing in My name; ask and you will receive, so that your joy may be made full (John 16:23–24 NASB).

REFLECT

_____

_____

_____

_____

Day 2. Ask and it will be given to you; seek and you will find; knock and the door will be opened to you (Matt. 7:7 NIV).

REFLECT

_____

_____

_____

_____

Day 3. And we will receive from him whatever we ask because we obey him and do the things that please him (1 John 3:22 NLT).

REFLECT

_____

_____

_____

_____

Day 4. Through faith in the name of Jesus, this man was healed—and you know how crippled he was before. Faith in Jesus's name has healed him before your very eyes (Acts 3:16 NLT).

REFLECT

_____

_____

_____

_____

Day 5. Therefore confess your sins to each other and pray for each other so that you may be healed. The prayer of a righteous man is powerful and effective (James 5:16 NIV).

REFLECT

_____

_____

_____

_____

Day 6. Use the following space to write any thoughts God has put in your heart and mind about the things we have looked at in this session and during your *Reflections* time.

SUMMARY

_____

_____

_____

_____

PERSISTENCE IN PRAYER
NEVER STOP BELIEVING

Memory Verse: And will not God bring about justice for his chosen ones, who cry out to him day and night? (Luke 18:7 NIV).

A small group of young Christians made a special effort to provide a Christmas Eve service for residents of a convalescent home. A few seniors hobbled in and others arrived in wheelchairs. The service went well, and at the end a whiskered man raised a feeble arm to receive Christ into his heart. Overjoyed, the team led him to Jesus.

In one corner a white-haired lady sat crying. Concerned, a young woman from the team approached her and asked what was wrong. "That's my husband," the lady sobbed. "I've been praying forty years for him to accept the Lord." Her tears were tears of joy!

Prayer requires persistence, especially in the face of long term, discouraging circumstances. The message is clear: Never give up praying. Even if it seems no answer is forthcoming, trust God, pray, and watch him work in his own timing.

Connecting

While we see immediate answers to some prayers, we must wait patiently on the Lord for answers to others. While we wait, we must lean on our Christian family for support and encouragement. Open your group in prayer, asking God to help group members encourage one another to pray persistently and never stop believing.

1. Share one thing that you learned about yourself or God as a result of this study that you will begin to apply in your own life.

2. Take time in this final session to connect with your spiritual partner. Turn to the *Personal Health Plan* and consider the "HOW are you surrendering your heart?" question. What has God been showing you through these sessions about prayer? Check in with each other about the progress you have made in your spiritual growth during this study. Talk about whether you might continue in your mentoring relationships outside your Bible study group.

Growing

The parable of the Persistent Widow in Luke 18 demonstrates the need for, and results of, persistence in our prayers to the One who can affect evil, suffering, and the need for justice in the world.

3. According to Luke 18:1, why did Jesus tell this parable?

   Is this an issue that you find challenging personally? Please explain.

4. Read Luke 18:2–5. A judge was supposed to fear God, defend the oppressed, and enforce justice. A widow was an oppressed person because she had no means of support. What do you think the widow's repeated appearances before the judge say about her?

5. The widow's adversary is presumably threatening something serious—widows and the fatherless were the most defenseless members of society and often the most exploited. Have you ever felt like you were in a similar situation? Please explain.

6. At first the judge ignores the widow's pleas for help but later changes his mind. How is the judge like or unlike God?

7. Read Luke 18:6–8. What is the main lesson Jesus wants us to learn from this story? Are there other lessons to be learned?

8. Why do you suppose God makes us wait and rewards persistence?

9. How have you seen God respond to persistent prayers? Talk about some examples out of your own life or from the Bible.

10. Jesus concludes the parable in verse 8b with an interesting statement: "However, when the Son of Man comes, will he find faith on the earth?" (NIV). What do you think Jesus means here?

11. How might the lessons in this parable change your attitude about prayer?

God desires our faithfulness and persistence in our prayers—no matter what—because he longs to see us wholly dependent upon him.

Developing

Persistent prayer helps us develop patience with ourselves and with others who are still growing in their faith. Commitment to praying for your group and its members will help you grow spiritually as you continue to grow together over time.

12. If you haven't already done so, take time to discuss the future of your group. What's next for your group? Will you continue to meet together? If so, the *Small Group Agreement* can help

you talk through any changes you might want to make as you move forward.

Surrendering

When humanly impossible situations are bathed in prayer and worship, you will be amazed at what God will do. Invite the Lord's presence among you, remembering that he is present when two or three are gathered in his name. Focus on God's goodness, his grace, and his patience with us in our long-term struggles.

13. Spend a few minutes reflecting on your own circumstances. Is there a situation that seems impossible? Have you given up praying about it? Pair up with your spiritual partner and offer that situation up to the Lord right now. You don't have to share any details in order to pray in agreement with one another. You can simply pray. The Lord already knows what you're facing.

14. Close by praying for your personal requests and take a couple of minutes to review the praises you have recorded over the course of this study on the *Prayer and Praise Report*. Thank God for what he's done in your group during this study.

Reflections

Each day, read the daily verses and give prayerful consideration to what you learn about God, his Spirit, and his place in your life. Then record your thoughts, insights, or prayer in the *Reflect* section below the verses you read. On the sixth day record a summary of what you have learned through this study session.

Day 1. Don't worry about anything; instead, pray about everything. Tell God what you need, and thank him for all he has done (Phil. 4:6 NLT).

REFLECT

_____

_____

_____

_____

Day 2. And pray in the Spirit on all occasions with all kinds of prayers and requests. With this in mind, be alert and always keep on praying for all the saints (Eph. 6:18 NIV).

REFLECT

_____

_____

_____

_____

Day 3. Be joyful always; pray continually; give thanks in all circumstances, for this is God's will for you in Christ Jesus (1 Thess. 5:16–18 NIV).

REFLECT

_____

_____

_____

_____

Day 4. Be merciful to me, O Lord, for I am calling on you constantly (Ps. 86:3 NLT).

REFLECT

_____

_____

_____

_____

Day 5. And so I tell you, keep on asking, and you will receive what you ask for. Keep on seeking, and you will find. Keep on knocking, and the door will be opened to you (Luke 11:9 NLT).

REFLECT

_____

_____

_____

_____

Day 6. Use the following space to write any thoughts God has put in your heart and mind about the things we have looked at in this session and during your _Reflections_ time.

SUMMARY

_____

_____

_____

_____

FREQUENTLY ASKED QUESTIONS

What do we do on the first night of our group?

Like all fun things in life—have a party! A "get to know you" coffee, dinner, or dessert is a great way to launch a new study. You may want to review the *Small Group Agreement* and share the names of a few friends you can invite to join you. But most importantly, have fun before your study time begins.

Where do we find new members for our group?

This can be challenging, especially for new groups that have only a few people or for existing groups that lose a few people along the way. We encourage you to pray with your group and then brainstorm a list of people from work, church, your neighborhood, your children's school, family, the gym, and so forth. Then have each group member invite several of the people on his or her list. Another good strategy is to ask church leaders to make an announcement that your group is open to new members.

No matter how you find members, it's vital that you stay on the lookout for new people to join your group. All groups tend to go through healthy attrition—the result of moves, releasing new leaders, ministry opportunities, and so forth—and if the group gets too small, it could be at risk of shutting down. If you and your group stay open, you'll be amazed at the people God sends your way. The next person just might become a friend for life. You never know!

How long will this group meet?

It's totally up to the group—once you come to the end of this study. Most groups meet weekly for at least their first six months together, but every other week can work as well. We strongly recommend that the group meet for the first six months on a weekly basis if at all possible. This allows for continuity, and if people miss a meeting they aren't gone for a whole month.

At the end of this study, each group member may decide whether he or she wants to continue on for another study. Some groups launch relationships that last for years, and others are stepping-stones into another group experience. Either way, enjoy the journey.

What if this group is not working for me?

Personality conflicts, life stage differences, geographical distance, level of spiritual maturity, or any number of things can cause you to feel the group doesn't work for you. Relax. Pray for God's direction, and at the end of this study decide whether to continue with this group or find another. You don't buy the first car you look at or marry the first person you date, and the same goes with a group. Don't bail out before the study is finished—God might have something to teach you. Also, don't run from conflict or prejudge people before you have given them a chance. God is still working in you too!

Who is the leader?

Most groups have an official leader. But ideally, the group will mature and members will share the facilitation of meetings. We have discovered that healthy groups share hosting and leading of the group. This model ensures that all members grow, give their unique contribution, and develop their gifts. This study guide and the Holy Spirit can keep things on track even when you share leadership. Christ has promised to be in your midst as you gather. Ultimately, God is your leader each step of the way.

How do we handle the child care needs in our group?

This can be a sensitive issue. We suggest that you empower the group to openly brainstorm solutions. You may try one option that works for a while and then adjust over time. Our favorite approach is for adults to meet in the living room or dining room, and share the cost of a babysitter (or two) who can be with the kids in a different part of the house. In this way, parents don't have to be away from their children all evening when their children are too young to be left at home. A second option is to use one home for the kids and a second home (close by) for the adults. A third idea is to rotate the responsibility of providing a lesson or care for the children either in the same home or in another home nearby. This can be an incredible blessing for kids. Finally, the most common idea is to decide that you need to have a night to invest in your spiritual lives individually or as a couple, and make your own arrangements for child care. No matter what decision the group makes, the best approach is to dialogue openly about both the problem and the solution.

SMALL GROUP AGREEMENT

Our Purpose

To transform our spiritual lives by cultivating our spiritual health in a healthy small group community. In addition, we:

_____

_____

_____

Our Values

Group Attendance	To give priority to the group meeting. We will call or e-mail if we will be late or absent. (Completing the *Small Group Calendar* will minimize this issue.)
Safe Environment	To help create a safe place where people can be heard and feel loved. (Please, no quick answers, snap judgments, or simple fixes.)
Respect Differences	To be gentle and gracious to people with different spiritual maturity, personal opinions, temperaments, or imperfections. We are all works in progress.
Confidentiality	To keep anything that is shared strictly confidential and within the group, and avoid sharing improper information about those outside the group.
Encouragement for Growth	To be not just takers but givers of life. We want to spiritually multiply our lives by serving others with our God-given gifts.

Welcome for Newcomers	To keep an open chair and share Jesus's dream of finding a shepherd for every sheep.
Shared Ownership	To remember that every member is a minister and to ensure that each attender will share a small team role or responsibility over time. (See the *Team Roles*.)
Rotating Hosts/ Leaders and Homes	To encourage different people to host the group in their homes, and to rotate the responsibility of facilitating each meeting. (See the *Small Group Calendar*.)

Our Expectations

- Refreshments/mealtimes _____
- Child care _____
- When we will meet (day of week) _____
- Where we will meet (place) _____
- We will begin at (time) _____ and end at _____
- We will do our best to have some or all of us attend a worship service together. Our primary worship service time will be _____
- Date of this agreement _____
- Date we will review this agreement again _____
- Who (other than the leader) will review this agreement at the end of this study _____

TEAM ROLES

The Bible makes clear that every member, not just the small group leader, is a minister in the body of Christ. In a healthy small group, every member takes on some small role or responsibility. It can be more fun and effective if you team up on these roles.

Review the team roles and responsibilities below, and have each member volunteer for a role or participate on a team. If someone doesn't know where to serve or is holding back, as a group, suggest a team or role. It's best to have one or two people on each team so you have each of the five purposes covered. Serving in even a small capacity will not only help your leader but also will make the group more fun for everyone. Don't hold back. Join a team!

The opportunities below are broken down by the five purposes and then by a *crawl* (beginning), *walk* (intermediate), or *run* (advanced) role. Try to cover at least the crawl and walk roles, and select a role that matches your group, your gifts, and your maturity.

Team Roles	Team Player(s)

CONNECTING TEAM (Fellowship and Community Building)

Crawl: Host a social event or group activity in the first week or
two. _____

Walk: Create a list of uncommitted friends and then invite them
to an open house or group social. _____

Run: Plan a twenty-four-hour retreat or weekend getaway for the
group. Lead the *Connecting* time each week for the group. _____

GROWING TEAM (Discipleship and Spiritual Growth)

Crawl: Coordinate the spiritual partners for the group. Facilitate
a three- or four-person discussion circle during the Bible study
portion of your meeting. Coordinate the discussion circles. _____

Walk: Tabulate the *Personal Health Plans* in a summary to let
people know how you're doing as a group. Encourage personal devotions through group discussions and pairing up
with spiritual (accountability) partners. _____

Run: Take the group on a prayer walk, or plan a day of solitude,
fasting, or personal retreat. _____

SERVING TEAM (Discovering Your God-Given Design for Ministry)

Crawl: Ensure that every member finds a group role or team he
or she enjoys. _____

Walk: Have every member take a gift test and determine your
group's gifts. Plan a ministry project together. _____

Run: Help each member decide on a way to use his or her unique
gifts somewhere in the church. _____

SHARING TEAM (Sharing and Evangelism)

Crawl: Coordinate the group's *Prayer and Praise Report* of
friends and family who don't know Christ. _____

Walk: Search for group mission opportunities and plan a cross-
cultural group activity. _____

Run: Take a small group "vacation" to host a six-week group in
your neighborhood or office. Then come back together with
your current group. _____

SURRENDERING TEAM (Surrendering Your Heart to Worship)

Crawl: Maintain the group's *Prayer and Praise Report* or
journal. _____

Walk: Lead a brief time of worship each week (at the beginning
or end of your meeting). _____

Run: Plan a more unique time of worship. _____

51

SMALL GROUP CALENDAR

Planning and calendaring can help ensure the greatest participation at every meeting. At the end of each meeting, review this calendar. Be sure to include a regular rotation of host homes and leaders, and don't forget birthdays, socials, church events, holidays, and mission/ministry projects.

Date	Lesson	Dessert/Meal	Role

PERSONAL HEALTH ASSESSMENT

	Just Beginning	Getting Going	Well Developed
CONNECTING with God's Family			
I am deepening my understanding of and friendship with God in community with others.		1 2 3 4 5	
I am growing in my ability both to share and to show my love to others.		1 2 3 4 5	
I am willing to share my real needs for prayer and support from others.		1 2 3 4 5	
I am resolving conflict constructively and am willing to forgive others.		1 2 3 4 5	
CONNECTING Total		_____	
GROWING to Be Like Christ			
I have a growing relationship with God through regular time in the Bible and in prayer (spiritual habits).		1 2 3 4 5	
I am experiencing more of the characteristics of Jesus Christ (love, patience, gentleness, courage, self-control, etc.) in my life.		1 2 3 4 5	
I am avoiding addictive behaviors (food, television, busyness, and the like) to meet my needs.		1 2 3 4 5	
I am spending time with a Christian friend (spiritual partner) who celebrates and challenges my spiritual growth.		1 2 3 4 5	
GROWING Total		_____	

53

	Just Beginning	Getting Going	Well Developed

DEVELOPING Your Gifts to Serve Others

I have discovered and am further developing my unique God-given design. 1 2 3 4 5

I am regularly praying for God to show me opportunities to serve him and others. 1 2 3 4 5

I am serving in a regular (once a month or more) ministry in the church or community. 1 2 3 4 5

I am a team player in my small group by sharing some group role or responsibility. 1 2 3 4 5

DEVELOPING Total _____

SHARING Your Life Mission Every Day

I am cultivating relationships with non-Christians and praying for God to give me natural opportunities to share his love. 1 2 3 4 5

I am praying and learning about where God can use me and our group cross-culturally for missions. 1 2 3 4 5

I am investing my time in another person or group who needs to know Christ. 1 2 3 4 5

I am regularly inviting unchurched or unconnected friends to my church or small group. 1 2 3 4 5

SHARING Total _____

SURRENDERING Your Life for God's Pleasure

I am experiencing more of the presence and power of God in my everyday life. 1 2 3 4 5

I am faithfully attending services and my small group to worship God. 1 2 3 4 5

I am seeking to please God by surrendering every area of my life (health, decisions, finances, relationships, future, etc.) to him. 1 2 3 4 5

I am accepting the things I cannot change and becoming increasingly grateful for the life I've been given. 1 2 3 4 5

SURRENDERING Total _____

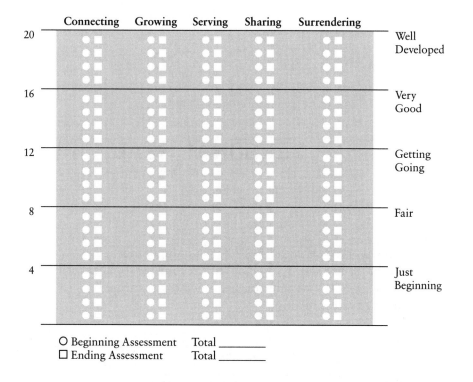

	Connecting	Growing	Serving	Sharing	Surrendering	
20						Well Developed
16						Very Good
12						Getting Going
8						Fair
4						Just Beginning

O Beginning Assessment   Total _____
□ Ending Assessment   Total _____

PERSONAL HEALTH PLAN

This worksheet could become your single most important feature in this study. On it you can record your personal priorities before the Father. It will help you live a healthy spiritual life, balancing all five of God's purposes.

PURPOSE	PLAN
CONNECT	WHO are you connecting with spiritually?
GROW	WHAT is your next step for growth?
DEVELOP	WHERE are you serving?
SHARE	WHEN are you shepherding another in Christ?
SURRENDER	HOW are you surrendering your heart to God?

DATE	MY PROGRESS	PARTNER'S PROGRESS

Personal Health Plan

DATE	MY PROGRESS	PARTNER'S PROGRESS

SAMPLE PERSONAL HEALTH PLAN

This worksheet could become your single most important feature in this study. On it you can record your personal priorities before the Father. It will help you live a healthy spiritual life, balancing all five of God's purposes.

PURPOSE	PLAN
CONNECT	WHO are you connecting with spiritually?
	Bill and I will meet weekly by e-mail or phone
GROW	WHAT is your next step for growth?
	Regular devotions or journaling my prayers 2×/week
DEVELOP	WHERE are you serving?
	Serving in children's ministry Go through GIFTS Assessment
SHARE	WHEN are you shepherding another in Christ?
	Shepherding Bill at lunch or hosting a starter group in the fall
SURRENDER	HOW are you surrendering your heart?
	Help with our teenager New job situation

DATE	MY PROGRESS	PARTNER'S PROGRESS
3/5	Talked during our group	Figured out our goals together
3/12	Missed our time together	Missed our time together
3/26	Met for coffee and review of my goals	Met for coffee
4/10	E-mailed prayer requests	Bill sent me his prayer requests
5/5	Great start on personal journaling	Read Mark 1–6 in one sitting!
5/12	Traveled and not doing well this week	Journaled about Christ as healer
5/26	Back on track	Busy and distracted; asked for prayer
6/1	Need to call Children's Pastor	
6/26	Group did a serving project together	Agreed to lead group worship
6/30	Regularly rotating leadership	Led group worship–great job!
7/5	Called Jim to see if he's open to joining our group	Wanted to invite somebody, but didn't
7/12	Preparing to start a group in fall	
7/30	Group prayed for me	Told friend something I'm learning about Christ
8/5	Overwhelmed but encouraged	Scared to lead worship
8/15	Felt heard and more settled	Issue with wife
8/30	Read book on teens	Glad he took on his fear

SPIRITUAL GIFTS INVENTORY

A spiritual gift is given to each of us as a means of helping the entire church.

1 Corinthians 12:7 (NLT)

A spiritual gift is a special ability, given by the Holy Spirit to every believer at their conversion. Although spiritual gifts are given when the Holy Spirit enters new believers, their use and purpose need to be understood and developed as we grow spiritually. A spiritual gift is much like a muscle; the more you use it, the stronger it becomes.

A Few Truths about Spiritual Gifts

1. Only believers have spiritual gifts. 1 Corinthians 2:14
2. You can't earn or work for a spiritual gift. Ephesians 4:7
3. The Holy Spirit decides what gifts I get. 1 Corinthians 12:11
4. I am to develop the gifts God gives me. Romans 11:29; 2 Timothy 1:6
5. It's a sin to waste the gifts God gave me. 1 Corinthians 4:1–2; Matthew 25:14–30
6. Using my gifts honors God and expands me. John 15:8

Gifts Inventory

God wants us to know what spiritual gift(s) he has given us. One person can have many gifts. The goal is to find the areas in which the Holy Spirit seems to have supernaturally empowered our service to others. These gifts are to be used to minister to others and build up the body of Christ.

There are four main lists of gifts found in the Bible in Romans 12:3–8; 1 Corinthians 12:1–11, 27–31; Ephesians 4:11–12; and 1 Peter 4:9–11. There are other passages that mention or illustrate gifts not included in these lists. As you read through this list, prayerfully consider whether the biblical definition describes you. Remember, you can have more than one gift, but everyone has at least one.

ADMINISTRATION (Organization)—1 Corinthians 12

This is the ability to recognize the gifts of others and recruit them to a ministry. It is the ability to organize and manage people, resources, and time for effective ministry.

APOSTLE—1 Corinthians 12

This is the ability to start new churches/ventures and oversee their development.

DISCERNMENT—1 Corinthians 12

This is the ability to distinguish between the spirit of truth and the spirit of error; to detect inconsistencies in another's life and confront in love.

ENCOURAGEMENT (Exhortation)—Romans 12

This is the ability to motivate God's people to apply and act on biblical principles, especially when they are discouraged or wavering in their faith. It is also the ability to bring out the best in others and challenge them to develop their potential.

EVANGELISM—Ephesians 4

This is the ability to communicate the gospel of Jesus Christ to unbelievers in a positive, nonthreatening way and to sense opportunities to share Christ and lead people to respond with faith.

FAITH—1 Corinthians 12

This is the ability to trust God for what cannot be seen and to act on God's promise, regardless of what the circumstances indicate. This includes a willingness to risk failure in pursuit of a God-given vision, expecting God to handle the obstacles.

GIVING—Romans 12

This is the ability to generously contribute material resources and/or money beyond the 10 percent tithe so that the church may grow and be strengthened. It includes the ability to manage money so it may be given to support the ministry of others.

HOSPITALITY—1 Peter 4:9–10

This is the ability to make others, especially strangers, feel warmly welcomed, accepted, and comfortable in the church family and the ability to coordinate factors that promote fellowship.

LEADERSHIP—Romans 12

This is the ability to clarify and communicate the purpose and direction ("vision") of a ministry in a way that attracts others to get involved, including the ability to motivate others, by example, to work together in accomplishing a ministry goal.

MERCY—Romans 12

This is the ability to manifest practical, compassionate, cheerful love toward suffering members of the body of Christ.

PASTORING (Shepherding)—Ephesians 4

This is the ability to care for the spiritual needs of a group of believers and equip them for ministry. It is also the ability to nurture a small group in spiritual growth and assume responsibility for their welfare.

PREACHING—Romans 12

This is the ability to publicly communicate God's Word in an inspired way that convinces unbelievers and both challenges and comforts believers.

SERVICE—Romans 12

This is the ability to recognize unmet needs in the church family, and take the initiative to provide practical assistance quickly, cheerfully, and without a need for recognition.

TEACHING—Ephesians 4

This is the ability to educate God's people by clearly explaining and applying the Bible in a way that causes them to learn; it is the ability to equip and train other believers for ministry.

WISDOM—1 Corinthians 12

This is the ability to understand God's perspective on life situations and share those insights in a simple, understandable way.

TELLING YOUR STORY

First, don't underestimate the power of your testimony. Revelation 12:11 says, "They have defeated [Satan] by the blood of the Lamb and by their testimony. And they did not love their lives so much that they were afraid to die" (NLT).

A simple three-point approach is very effective in communicating your personal testimony. The approach focuses on before you trusted Christ, how you surrendered to him, and the difference in you since you've been walking with him. If you became a Christian at a very young age and don't remember what life was like before Christ, reflect on what you have seen in the lives of others. Before you begin, pray and ask God to give you the right words.

Before You Knew Christ

Simply tell what your life was like before you surrendered to Christ. What was the key problem, emotion, situation, or attitude you were dealing with? What motivated you? What were your actions? How did you try to satisfy your inner needs? Create an interesting picture of your preconversion life and problems, and then explain what created a need and interest in Christian things.

How You Came to Know Christ

How were you converted? Simply tell the events and circumstances that caused you to consider Christ as the solution to your needs. Take time to identify the steps that brought you to the point of trusting Christ. Where were you? What was happening at the time? What people or problems influenced your decision?

The Difference Christ Has Made in Your Life

What is different about your life in Christ? How has his forgiveness impacted you? How have your thoughts, attitudes, and emotions changed? What problems have been resolved or changed? Share how Christ is meeting your needs and what a relationship with him means to you now. This should be the largest part of your story.

Tips

- Don't use jargon: don't sound churchy, preachy, or pious.
- Stick to the point. Your conversion and new life in Christ should be the main points.
- Be specific. Include events, genuine feelings, and personal insights, both before and after conversion, which people would be interested in and that clarify your main point. This makes your testimony easier to relate to. Assume you are sharing with someone with no knowledge of the Christian faith.
- Be current. Tell what is happening in your life with God now, today.
- Be honest. Don't exaggerate or portray yourself as living a perfect life with no problems. This is not realistic. The simple truth of what God has done in your life is all the Holy Spirit needs to convict someone of their sin and convince them of his love and grace.
- Remember, it's the Holy Spirit who convicts. You need only be obedient and tell your story.
- When people reply to your efforts to share with statements like "I don't believe in God," "I don't believe the Bible is God's Word," or "How can a loving God allow suffering?" how can we respond to these replies?

- Above all, keep a positive attitude. Don't be defensive.
- Be sincere. This will speak volumes about your confidence in your faith.
- Don't be offended. It's not you they are rejecting.
- Pray—silently on-the-spot. Don't proceed without asking for God's help about the specific question. Seek his guidance on how, or if, you should proceed at this time.
- In God's wisdom, choose to do one of the following:
  - Postpone sharing at this time.
  - Answer their objections, if you can.
  - Promise to research their questions and return answers later.

Step 1. Everywhere Jesus went he used stories, or parables, to demonstrate our need for salvation. Through these stories, he helped people see the error of their ways, leading them to turn to him. Your story can be just as powerful today. Begin to develop your story by sharing what your life was like before you knew Christ. (If you haven't yet committed your life to Christ, or became a Christian at a very young age and don't remember what life was like before Christ, reflect on what you have seen in the life of someone close to you.) Make notes about this aspect of your story below and commit to writing it out this week.

_____

_____

_____

Step 2. Sit in groups of two or three people for this discussion. Review the "How You Came to Know Christ" section. Begin to develop this part of your story by sharing within your circle. Make notes about this aspect of your story below and commit to writing it out this week.

_____

_____

_____

Step 2b. Connecting: Go around the group and share about a time you were stopped cold while sharing Christ, by a question you couldn't answer. What happened?

Step 2c. Sharing: Previously we talked about the questions and objections we receive that stop us from continuing to share our faith with someone. These questions/objections might include:

- "I don't believe in God."
- "I don't believe the Bible is God's Word."
- "How can a loving God allow suffering?"

How can we respond to these replies?

Step 3. Subgroup into groups of two or three people for this discussion. Review "The Difference Christ Has Made in Your Life" section. Share the highlights of this part of your story within your circle. Make notes about this aspect of your story below and commit to writing it out this week.

_____

_____

_____

Step 3b. Story: There's nothing more exciting than a brand-new believer. My wife became a Christian four years before I met her. She was a flight attendant at the time. Her zeal to introduce others to Jesus was reminiscent of the woman at the well who ran and got the whole town out to see Jesus.

My wife immediately began an international organization of Christian flight attendants for fellowship and for reaching out to others in their profession. She organized events where many people came to Christ, and bid for trips with another flight attendant who was a Christian so they could witness on the planes. They even bid for the shorter trips so they could talk to as many different people as possible. They had a goal for every flight to talk to at least one person about Christ, and to be encouraged by at least one person who already knew him. God met that request every time.

In her zeal, however, she went home to her family over the holidays and vacations and had little or no success. Later she would realize that she pressed them too hard. Jesus said a prophet is without honor in his own town, and I think the same goes for family. That's because members of your family think they know you, and are more likely to ignore changes, choosing instead to see you as they've always seen you. "Isn't this the carpenter's son—the son of Joseph?" they said of Jesus. "Don't we know this guy?"

With family members you have to walk with Christ openly and be patient. Change takes time. And remember, we don't save anyone. We just introduce them to Jesus through telling our own story. God does the rest.

Step 4. As a group, review *Telling Your Story*. Share which part of your story is the most difficult for you to tell. Which is the easiest for you? If you have time, a few of you share your story with the group.

Step 5. Throughout this study we have had the opportunity to develop our individual testimonies. One way your group can serve each other is to provide a safe forum for "practicing" telling your stories. Continue to take turns sharing your testimonies now. Set a time limit—say two to three minutes each. Don't miss this great opportunity to get to know one another better and encourage each other's growth too.

SERVING COMMUNION

Churches vary in their treatment of communion (or the Lord's Supper). We offer one simple form by which a small group can share this experience together. You can adapt this as necessary, or omit it from your group altogether, depending on your church's beliefs.

Steps in Serving Communion

1. Open by sharing about God's love, forgiveness, grace, mercy, commitment, tenderheartedness, faithfulness, etc., out of your personal journey (connect with the stories of those in the room).
2. Read one or several of the passages listed below.
3. Pray and pass the bread around the circle.
4. When everyone has been served, remind them that this represents Jesus's broken body on their behalf. Simply state, "Jesus said, 'Do this in remembrance of me' (Luke 22:19 NIV). Let us eat together," and eat the bread as a group.
5. Then read the rest of the passage: "In the same way, after the supper he took the cup, saying, 'This cup is the new covenant in my blood, which is poured out for you'" (Luke 22:20 NIV).
6. Pray, and serve the cups, either by passing a small tray, serving them individually, or having members pick up a cup from the table.
7. When everyone has been served, remind them the juice represents Christ's blood shed for them, then simply state, "Take and drink in remembrance of him. Let us drink together."
8. Finish by singing a simple song, listening to a praise song, or having a time of prayer in thanks to God.

Communion passages: Matthew 26:26–29; Mark 14:22–25; Luke 22:14–20; 1 Corinthians 10:16–21; 11:17–34.

PERFORMING A FOOTWASHING

Scripture: John 13:1–17. Jesus makes it quite clear to his disciples that his position as the Father's Son includes being a servant rather than power and glory only. To properly understand the scene and the intention of Jesus, we must realize that the washing of feet was the duty of slaves and indeed of non-Jewish rather than Jewish slaves. Jesus placed himself in the position of a servant. He displayed to the disciples self-sacrifice and love. In view of his majesty, only the symbolic position of a slave was adequate to open their eyes and keep them from lofty illusions. The point of footwashing, then, is to correct the attitude that Jesus discerned in the disciples. It constitutes the permanent basis for mutual service, service in your group and for the community around you, which is the responsibility of all Christians.

When to Implement

There are three primary places we would recommend you insert a footwashing: during a break in the Surrendering section of your group; during a break in the Growing section of your group; or at the closing of your group. A special time of prayer for each person as he or she gets his or her feet washed can be added to the footwashing time.

SURRENDERING AT THE CROSS

Surrendering everything to God is one of the most challenging aspects of following Jesus. It involves a relationship built on trust and faith. Each of us is in a different place on our spiritual journey. Some of us have known the Lord for many years, some are new in our faith, and some may still be checking God out. Regardless, we all have things that we still want control over—things we don't want to give to God because we don't know what he will do with them. These things are truly more important to us than God is—they have become our god.

We need to understand that God wants us to be completely devoted to him. If we truly love God with all our heart, soul, strength, and mind (Luke 10:27), we will be willing to give him everything.

Steps in Surrendering at the Cross

1. You will need some small pieces of paper and pens or pencils for people to write down the things they want to sacrifice/surrender to God.
2. If you have a wooden cross, hammers, and nails you can have the members nail their sacrifices to the cross. If you don't have a wooden cross, get creative. Think of another way to symbolically relinquish the sacrifices to God. You might use a fireplace to burn them in the fire as an offering to the Lord. The point is giving to the Lord whatever hinders your relationship with him.

3. Create an atmosphere conducive to quiet reflection and prayer. Whatever this quiet atmosphere looks like for your group, do the best you can to create a peaceful time to meet with God.

4. Once you are settled, prayerfully think about the points below. Let the words and thoughts draw you into a heart-to-heart connection with your Lord Jesus Christ.

☐ *Worship him.* Ask God to change your viewpoint so you can worship him through a surrendered spirit.

☐ *Humble yourself.* Surrender doesn't happen without humility. James 4:6–7 says: "'God opposes the proud but gives grace to the humble.' Submit yourselves, then, to God" (NIV).

☐ *Surrender your mind, will, and emotions.* This is often the toughest part of surrendering. What do you sense God urging you to give him so you can have the kind of intimacy he desires with you? Our hearts yearn for this kind of connection with him; let go of the things that stand between you.

☐ *Write out your prayer.* Write out your prayer of sacrifice and surrender to the Lord. This may be an attitude, a fear, a person, a job, a possession—anything that God reveals is a hindrance to your relationship with him.

5. After writing out your sacrifice, take it to the cross and offer it to the Lord. Nail your sacrifice to the cross, or burn it as a sacrifice in the fire.

6. Close by singing, praying together, or taking communion. Make this time as short or as long as seems appropriate for your group.

Surrendering to God is life-changing and liberating. God desires that we be overcomers! First John 4:4 says, "You, dear children, are from God and have overcome . . . because the one who is in you is greater than the one who is in the world" (NIV).

JOURNALING 101

Henri Nouwen says effective and lasting ministry *for* God grows out of a quiet place alone *with* God. This is why journaling is so important.

The greatest adventure of our lives is found in the daily pursuit of knowing, growing in, serving, sharing, and worshiping Christ forever. This is the essence of a purposeful life: to see all these biblical purposes fully formed and balanced in our lives. Only then are we "complete in Christ" (Col. 1:28 NASB).

David poured his heart out to God by writing psalms. The book of Psalms contains many of his honest conversations with God in written form, including expressions of every imaginable emotion on every aspect of his life. Like David, we encourage you to select a strategy to integrate God's Word and journaling into your devotional time. Use any of the following resources:

- Bible
- Bible reading plan
- Devotional
- Topical Bible study plan

Before and after you read a portion of God's Word, speak to God in honest reflection in the form of a written prayer. You may begin this time by simply finishing the sentence "Father, . . . ," "Yesterday, Lord, . . . ," or "Thank you, God, for, ..." Share with him where you are at the present moment; express your hurts, disappointments, frustrations, blessings, victories, and gratefulness. Whatever you do with your journal, make a plan that fits you, so you'll have a positive experience. Consider sharing highlights of your progress and experiences with some or all of your group members, especially your spiritual partner. You may find they want to join and even encourage you in this journey. Most of all, enjoy the ride and cultivate a more authentic, growing walk with God.

PRAYER AND PRAISE REPORT

Briefly share your prayer requests with the large group, making notations below. Then gather in small groups of two to four to pray for each other.

Date: _____

Prayer Requests

_____

_____

_____

_____

_____

Praise Reports

_____

_____

_____

_____

_____

Prayer and Praise Report

Briefly share your prayer requests with the large group, making notations below. Then gather in small groups of two to four to pray for each other.

Date: _____

Prayer Requests

_____
_____
_____
_____
_____

Praise Reports

_____
_____
_____
_____
_____

Prayer and Praise Report

Briefly share your prayer requests with the large group, making notations below. Then gather in small groups of two to four to pray for each other.

Date: _____

Prayer Requests

_____
_____
_____

_____

_____

Praise Reports

_____

_____

_____

_____

_____

Prayer and Praise Report

Briefly share your prayer requests with the large group, making notations below. Then gather in small groups of two to four to pray for each other.

Date: _____

Prayer Requests

_____

_____

_____

_____

_____

Praise Reports

_____

_____

_____

_____

_____

Prayer and Praise Report

Briefly share your prayer requests with the large group, making notations below. Then gather in small groups of two to four to pray for each other.

Date: _____

Prayer Requests

_____

_____

_____

_____

_____

Praise Reports

_____

_____

_____

_____

_____

SMALL GROUP ROSTER

Name	Address	Phone	E-mail Address	Team or Role	When/How to Contact You
Bill Jones	7 Alvalar Street L.F. 92665	766-2255	bjones@aol.com	Socials	Evenings After 5

(Pass your book around your group at your first meeting to get everyone's name and contact information.)

Name	Address	Phone	E-mail Address	Team or Role	When/How to Contact You

LEADING FOR THE FIRST TIME
LEADERSHIP 101

Sweaty palms are a healthy sign. The Bible says God is gracious to the humble. Remember who is in control; the time to worry is when you're not worried. Those who are soft in heart (and sweaty-palmed) are those whom God is sure to speak through.

Seek support. Ask your leader, coleader, or close friend to pray for you and prepare with you before the session. Walking through the study will help you anticipate potentially difficult questions and discussion topics.

Bring your uniqueness to the study. Lean into who you are and how God wants you to uniquely lead the study.

Prepare. Prepare. Prepare. Go through the session several times. If you are using the DVD, listen to the teaching segment and *Leader Lifter*. Consider writing in a journal or fasting for a day to prepare yourself for what God wants to do.

Don't wait until the last minute to prepare.

Ask for feedback so you can grow. Perhaps in an e-mail or on cards handed out at the study, have everyone write down three things you did well and one thing you could improve on. Don't get defensive, but show an openness to learn and grow.

Prayerfully consider launching a new group. This doesn't need to happen overnight, but God's heart is for this to happen over time. Not all Christians are called to be leaders or teachers, but we are all called to be "shepherds" of a few someday.

Share with your group what God is doing in your heart. God is searching for those whose hearts are fully his. Share your trials and victories. We promise that people will relate.

Prayerfully consider whom you would like to pass the baton to next week. It's only fair. God is ready for the next member of your group to go on the faith journey you just traveled. Make it fun, and expect God to do the rest.

LEADER'S NOTES
INTRODUCTION

Congratulations! You have responded to the call to help shepherd Jesus's flock. There are few other tasks in the family of God that surpass the contribution you will be making. We have provided you several ways to prepare for this role. Between the *Read Me First*, these *Leader's Notes*, and the *Watch This First* and *Leader Lifter* segments on the optional *Deepening Life Together: Praying God's Way* Video Teaching DVD, you'll have all you need to do a great job of leading your group. Just don't forget, you are not alone. God knew that you would be asked to lead this group and he won't let you down. In Hebrews 13:5b God promises us, "Never will I leave you; never will I forsake you" (NIV).

Your role as leader is to create a safe, warm environment for your group. As a leader, your most important job is to create an atmosphere where people are willing to talk honestly about what the topics discussed in this study have to do with them. Be available before people arrive so you can greet them at the door. People are naturally nervous at a new group, so a hug or handshake can help put them at ease. Before you start leading your group, a little preparation will give you confidence. Review the *Read Me First* at the front of your study guide so you'll understand the purpose of each section, enabling you to help your group understand it as well.

If you're new to leading a group, congratulations and thank you; this will be a life-changing experience for you also. We have provided these *Leader's Notes* to help new leaders begin well.

It's important in your first meeting to make sure group members understand that things shared personally and in prayer must remain confidential. Also, be careful not to dominate the group discussion, but facilitate it and encourage others to join in and share. And lastly, have fun.

Take a moment at the beginning of your first meeting to orient the group to one principle that undergirds this study: A healthy small group balances the purposes of the church. Most small groups emphasize Bible study, fellowship, and prayer. But God has called us to reach out to others as well. He wants us to do what Jesus teaches, not just learn about it.

Preparing for each meeting ahead of time. Take the time to review the session, the *Leader's Notes*, and *Leader Lifter* for the session before each session. Also write down your answers to each question. Pay special attention to exercises that ask group members to *do* something. These exercises will help your group live out what the Bible teaches, not just talk about it. Be sure you understand how the exercises work, and bring any supplies you might need, such as paper or pens. Pray for your group members by name at least once between sessions and before each session. Use the *Prayer and Praise Report* so you will remember their prayer requests. Ask God to use your time together to touch the heart of every person. Expect God to give you the opportunity to talk with those he wants you to encourage or challenge in a special way.

Don't try to go it alone. Pray for God to help you. Ask other members of your group to help by taking on some small role. In the *Appendix* you'll find the *Team Roles* pages with some suggestions to get people involved. Leading is more rewarding if you give group members opportunities to help. Besides, helping group members discover their individual gifts for serving or even leading the group will bless all of you.

Consider asking a few people to come early to help set up, pray, and introduce newcomers to others. Even if everyone is new, they don't know that yet and may be shy when they arrive. You might give people roles like setting up name tags or handing out drinks. This could be a great way to spot a co-leader.

Subgrouping. If your group has more than seven people, break into discussion groups of three to four people for the *Growing* and *Surrendering* sections each week. People will connect more with the study and each other when they have more opportunity to participate. Smaller discussion circles encourage quieter people to talk more and tend to minimize the effects of more vocal or dominant members. Also, people who are unaccustomed to praying aloud will feel more comfortable praying within a smaller group of people. Share prayer requests in the larger group and then break into smaller groups to pray for each other. People are more willing to pray in small circles if they know that the whole group will hear all the prayer requests.

Memorizing Scripture. At the start of each session you will find a memory verse—a verse for the group to memorize each week. Encourage your group members to do this. Memorizing God's Word is both directed and celebrated throughout the Bible, either explicitly ("Your word I have hidden in my heart, that I might not sin against You" [Ps. 119:11 NKJV]), or implicitly, as in the example of our Lord ("He departed to the mountain to pray" [Mark 6:46 NKJV]).

Anyone who has memorized Scripture can confirm the amazing spiritual benefits that result from this practice. Don't miss out on the opportunity to encourage your group to grow in the knowledge of God's Word through Scripture memorization.

Reflections. We've provided opportunity for a personal time with God using the *Reflections* at the end of each session. Don't press seekers to do this, but just remind the group that every believer should have a plan for personal time with God.

Inviting new people. Cast the vision, as Jesus did, to be inclusive not exclusive. Ask everyone to prayerfully think of people who would enjoy or benefit from a group like this—then invite them. The beginning of a new study is a great time to welcome a few people into your circle. Don't worry about ending up with too many people—you can always have one discussion circle in the living room and another in the dining room.

For Deeper Study (Optional). We have included a *For Deeper Study* section in each session. *For Deeper Study* provides additional passages for individual study on the topic of each session. If your group likes to do deeper Bible study, consider having members study the *For Deeper Study* passages for homework. Then, during the *Growing* portion of your meeting, you can share the high points of what you've learned.

LEADER'S NOTES

SESSIONS

Session One The Priority of Prayer

Connecting

1. We've designed this study for both new and established groups, and for both seekers and the spiritually mature. New groups need to invest more time building relationships with each other. Established groups often want to dig deeper into Bible study and application. Whether your group is new or has been together for a while, be sure to introduce yourselves to new people.

2. A very important item in this first session is the *Small Group Agreement*. An agreement helps clarify your group's priorities and cast new vision for what the group can become. You can find this in the *Appendix* of this study guide. We've found that groups that talk about these values up front and commit to an agreement benefit significantly. They work through conflicts long before people get to the point of frustration, so there's a lot less pain.

   Take some time to review this agreement before your meeting. Then during your meeting, read the agreement aloud to the entire group. If some people have concerns about a specific item or the agreement as a whole, be sensitive to their concerns. Explain that tens of thousands of groups use agreements like this one as a simple tool for building trust and group health over time.

   As part of this discussion, we recommend talking about shared ownership of the group. It's important that each member have a role. See the *Appendix* to learn more about *Team Roles*. This is a great tool to get this important practice launched in your group.

   Also, you will find a *Small Group Calendar* in the *Appendix* for use in planning your group meetings and roles. Take a look at the calendar prior to your first meeting and point it out to the group so that each person can note when and where the group will meet, who will bring snacks, any important upcoming events (birthdays, anniversaries), etc.

Growing

Have someone read Bible passages aloud. It's a good idea to ask ahead of time, because not everyone is comfortable reading aloud in public.

4. Jesus was a man of action, whose ministry was a whirlwind of teaching, healing, casting out demons, and proclaiming the kingdom of God.

5. Jesus had just had a successful ministry in Capernaum healing many sick and demon-possessed people. Early the next day, Jesus went out by himself for a time of prayer. By the time the disciples found him, he was ready to face the day. We must follow Christ's example by making time for personal prayer. Those who help and serve on Sunday especially need to set aside time with God to restore their strength. Our ability to serve will be hindered if we neglect times of spiritual replenishment. During his ministry on earth, Jesus was in constant prayer with the Father. Mark recorded three of these times (see Mark 6:46 and 14:32–42).

9. Jesus prayed at key transitions and crisis points in his life. For example, here he prayed as the Holy Spirit descended on him after his baptism. He also prayed in the Garden of Gethsemane (Luke 22:41–44) and even on the cross (Luke 23:46).

It's important to examine what specific things Jesus prayed about so we can do the same. First, Jesus prayed before making decisions such as in the case of choosing his twelve disciples. This should serve an example to us that we, like Jesus, need the strength and wisdom of the Father in our lives.

In Luke 22:41–44, Jesus prayed before going to the cross. In the garden Jesus's prayer was agonizing. Yet, his prayer brought clarity to his situation. In Luke 23:46, Jesus gave up his spirit and died.

Developing

This section enables you to help the group see the importance of developing our abilities for service to God.

13. For many, spiritual partners will be a new idea. We highly encourage you to try pairs for this study. It's so hard to start a spiritual practice like prayer or consistent Bible reading with no support. A friend makes a huge difference. As leader, you may want to prayerfully decide who would be a good match with whom. Remind people that this partnership isn't forever; it's just for a few weeks. Be sure to have extra copies of the *Personal Health Plan* available

at this meeting in case you need to have a group of three spiritual partners. It is a good idea for you to look over the Personal Health Plan before the meeting so you can help people understand how to use it.

Instruct your group members to enlist a spiritual partner by asking them to pair up with someone in the group (we suggest that men partner with men and women with women) and turn to the *Personal Health Plan*.

Ask the group to complete the instructions in the session for the WHO and WHAT questions on the *Personal Health Plan*. Your group has now begun to address two of God's purposes for their lives!

You can see that the *Personal Health Plan* contains space to record the ups and downs and progress over time in the column labeled "My Progress." When partners check in each meeting they can record their partner's progress in the goal he or she chose in the "Partner's Progress" column on this chart. In the *Appendix* you'll find a *Sample Personal Health Plan* filled in as an example.

The WHERE, WHEN, and HOW questions on the *Personal Health Plan* will be addressed in future sessions of the study.

Sharing

Jesus wants all of his disciples to help outsiders connect with him, to know him personally. This section should provide an opportunity to go beyond Bible study to biblical living.

14. We provided a *Circles of Life* diagram for you and the group to use to help you identify people who need to be connected in Christian community. When people are asked why they never go to church they often say, "No one ever invited me." Remind the group that our responsibility is to invite people, but we are not responsible for how they respond. Talk to the group about the importance of inviting people; remind them that healthy small groups make a habit of inviting friends, neighbors, unconnected church members, co-workers, etc., to join their groups or join them at a weekend service. When people get connected to a group of new friends they often join the church.

The *Circles of Life* represent one of the values of the *Small Group Agreement* "Welcome for Newcomers." Some groups fear that newcomers will interrupt the intimacy that members have built over time. However, groups generally gain strength with the infusion of new blood. It's like a river of living water flowing into a stagnant pond. Some groups remain permanently open, while others open periodically, such as at the beginning and ending of a study. Love grows by giving itself away. If your circle becomes too large for easy face-to-face conversations, you can simply form a second discussion circle in another room in your home.

Surrendering

God is most pleased by a heart that is fully his. Each group session will provide group members a chance to surrender their hearts to God in prayer and worship. Group prayer requests and prayer time should be included every meeting.

16. As you move to the time of sharing your prayer requests, be sure to remind the group of the importance of confidentiality and keeping what is shared in the group within the group. Everyone must feel that things will not go beyond the group if you are to have safety and bonding in the group.

    Use the *Prayer and Praise Report* in the *Appendix* to record your prayer requests. There you can keep track of requests and celebrate answers to prayer.

17. This question is meant to encourage quiet time at home each day throughout the week. Here you can help the group see the importance of making time with God a priority. Read through this section and be prepared to help the group understand how important it is to fill our minds with the Word of God. If people already have a good Bible reading plan and commitment, that is great, but you may have people who struggle to stay in the Word daily. Sometimes beginning with a simple commitment to a short daily reading can start a habit that changes their life. The *Reflections* pages at the end of each session include verses that were either talked about in the session or support the teaching of the session. They are very short readings with a few lines to encourage people to write down their thoughts. Remind the group about these *Reflections* each session after the *Surrendering* section.

For Deeper Study

We have included an optional *For Deeper Study* section in each session. *For Deeper Study* provides additional passages for individual study on the topic of each session. If your group likes to do deeper Bible study, consider having members study the *For Deeper Study* passages at home between meetings.

Session Two The Pattern of Prayer

Connecting

2. Turn to your *Personal Health Plan*. Share with your partner how your time with God went since the last meeting. What is one thing you discovered? Did you make a commitment to a next step that you can share? Make a note about your partner's progress and how you can pray for him or her.

Growing

The Lord's Prayer is not meant to be a ritual. Instead it takes us on an exciting journey of communication with God. There are three main sections to it. The first part gives the ultimate goal of prayer. The second offers provision for our life's journey, and the third promises God's protection along the way.

4. Right away in verse 9, Jesus expresses the ultimate goal of prayer: to glorify God, which means to acknowledge his greatness. When we address our prayer to the Father, we are declaring his greatness. "Hallowed" means "holy." When we pray, our understanding of his greatness grows. Jesus's prayer pattern was to praise God first. The phrase Our Father in heaven indicates that God is majestic and holy and transcends everything on earth. But he is also personal and loving (our Father). So the first line of this prayer is a statement of praise and a commitment to honor God's holy name. Christians must honor him in every aspect of their lives. When we pray for God's name to be honored, we pray that this world will honor his name, and we look forward to Christ's return when that will be a reality.

5. Jesus encouraged us to ask for God's rule to be established in the here and now, as it is in heaven. When we pray this, we affirm God's good plan and purpose for the world. We declare the surrender of our will to God in this prayer when we pray your will be done on earth as it is in heaven.

6. God cares about every detail of our lives, whether large or small. He knows we need sustenance to serve him well, and he doesn't discourage us from petitioning him to meet our physical needs each and every day. He wants us to develop a mental habit of awareness of daily, constant dependence on him.

7. Asking God to forgive our sins is essential to maintaining a right relationship with him. The word used in this verse is "debts," or sins. These are moral debts. Unconfessed sin separates us from God. Repentance and asking forgiveness is the way to become right with God.

8. Jesus gives the prerequisite for receiving forgiveness in verse 12: as we also have forgiven our debtors. The ability to freely forgive doesn't happen for most people overnight. An authentic relationship with God means that we gradually take on his character. And his character is one of love and forgiveness.

9. Jesus acknowledged the personal threat of evil and warned us to be vigilant in prayer about it. Insight and strength for how we respond to the temptation (trial) is what we are praying about.

10. There are many responses to suffering. Some of us worry and grumble about it; some of us seek revenge against those who have caused it; others of us

burn with anger. But James 5:13–16 says the correct response to suffering is to pray about it (see also Ps. 30; 50:15; 91:15). The Lord's Prayer models that. It's okay to pray for deliverance from the trouble, and we should also ask for the patience and strength to endure it. In the midst of suffering, we shouldn't lose sight of the fact that God is our Father, that he is holy, and that his will is more important to us than a pain-free life.

Developing

12. Here is an opportunity for group members to consider where they can take a next step toward getting involved in ministering to the body of Christ in your small group or in the church. Encourage group members to use the *Personal Health Plan* to jot down their next step and plan how and when they will begin.

13. Point the group to the *Spiritual Gifts Inventory* in the *Appendix*. Encourage them to read through these on their own time during the coming days and identify one or two that fits them. We will refer to this home exercise again in *Session Three*.

Sharing

14. We encourage an outward focus for your group because groups that become too inwardly-focused tend to become unhealthy over time. People naturally gravitate to feeding themselves through Bible study, prayer, and social time, so it's usually up to the leader to push them to consider how this inward nourishment can overflow into outward concern for others. Never forget: Jesus came to seek and save the lost and to find a shepherd for every sheep.

Session Three The Power of Prayer

Connecting

2. It's time to start thinking about what your group will do when you're finished with this study. Now is the time to ask how many people will be joining you so you can choose a study and have the books available when you meet for the next session.

Growing

4. In these words, Jesus reveals the heart of God the Father. If sinful people would not consider giving a child a stone that looked like bread or a danger-

ous snake instead of a fish, then how much more will a holy God acknowledge and answer our requests? God is not selfish, begrudging, or stingy. He is a loving Father who understands, cares, comforts, and willingly gives good gifts to those who ask him. However, many of us find it hard to see him that way, often because of our past experiences. It's good to express those thoughts aloud to trusted friends.

5. The Lord took the opportunity to teach about the power of faith joined to the purpose and will of God, so that the Father is glorified through the Son.

6. To pray "in Jesus's name" is to pray in union with Jesus's person and purpose. In ancient times, the "name" of a person symbolized his essence and destiny. We have the promise of answered prayer when what we ask for will bring glory to God and when we are inhabiting Jesus's words about what he wants done in the world.

7. Believers can be confident that God will listen to their prayers when they pray in line with his will (see also John 14:13–14; 15:16; 16:21–24). Asking in accordance with God's will requires faith and belief that God can and will answer—though sometimes the answer is not in accordance with our wishes. Jesus himself was a model of this: he taught his followers to pray for God's will to be accomplished on earth (Matt. 6:10), and he chose God's will over his own in accepting the cup—death on the cross (Matt. 26:39–42).

8. Jesus asks the Father to allow him not to drink the cup of suffering that awaits him. The Father says no to that request. Jesus also asks to put the Father's will ahead of that earlier request, and the Father grants that. Jesus prays boldly, trusting that the Father wants to know his heart. Jesus walks willingly into terrible suffering, trusting that the Father is good and so his will is good.

Developing

10. Discuss with the group how quiet times have been going. Which steps have been taken and how is it going? Encourage the group to commit to a next step in prayer, Bible reading, or meditation on the Word.

11. The group should have reviewed the *Spiritual Gifts Inventory* in preparation for this session. Discuss some specific action steps to take as a result of their discoveries.

Sharing

12. It is important to return to the *Circles of Life* and engage the group in identifying people who need to know Christ. Encourage a commitment to praying for God's guidance and an opportunity to share with each of them.

13. Encourage group members to turn to the *Personal Health Plan* and answer the question "WHEN are you shepherding another person in Christ?" Then, have them identify their next step and plan how and when they will begin.

Session Four Persistence in Prayer

Connecting

1. Whether your group is ending or continuing, it's important to celebrate where you have grown together. Take a few minutes for group members to share one thing they learned or a commitment they made or renewed during this study. They may also want to share what they enjoyed most about the study and about this group.

2. Be sure to have spiritual partners check in with each other at this last meeting. Encourage them to share where they have grown and where they would like to continue to grow.

Growing

6. Like many of Jesus's parables, this one contains an element intended to shock listeners into thinking. In this case we're challenged to ask, is God like this hardhearted judge? The answer is that their characters couldn't be more different. The point is that if this unworthy judge who feels no constraint of right or wrong can be compelled to act justly by persistence, how much more will a righteous judge, God, answer our prayers.

7. God is just, far more just than this judge, and he will respond to persistence. Also, note the references to justice. This parable assumes we're crying out for justice. Is that something you pray for?

10. The question Jesus is asking here is "will people have persisted in faith?" Will anyone be ready and waiting when he comes?

DEEPENING LIFE TOGETHER SERIES

Deepening Life Together is a series of Bible studies that offers small groups an opportunity to explore biblical subjects in several categories: books of the Bible (*Acts, Romans, John, Ephesians, Revelation*), theology (*Promises of God, Parables*), and spiritual disciplines (*Prayers of Jesus*).

A *Deepening Life Together* Video Teaching DVD companion is available for each study in the series. For each study session, the DVD contains a lesson taught by a master teacher backed by scholars giving their perspective on the subject.

Every study includes activities based on five biblical purposes of the church: Connecting, Growing, Developing, Sharing, and Surrendering. These studies will help your group deepen your walk with God while you discover what he has created you for and how you can turn his desires into an everyday reality in your lives. Experience the transformation firsthand as you begin deepening your life together.